WILBUR, ORVILLE

. . . AND SIMONE

WILBUR, ORVILLE
. . . AND SIMONE

The Seagull Who Helped the
Wright Brothers Learn to Fly

Bill Eckert

Library of Congress Control Number: 2016907897
ISBN: Hardcover   978-1-5245-0085-6
                 Softcover   978-1-5245-0084-9
                 eBook   978-1-5245-0083-2

Print information available on the last page

Rev. date: 05/16/2016

To order additional copies of this book, contact:
Xlibris
1-888-795-4274
www.Xlibris.com
Orders@Xlibris.com
742615

To My Wife Sue And Our Daughter Katie, Both Of Whom Have Flown In The Service Of Our Country.

This Book Is Historical Fiction.

CONTENTS

WILBUR, ORVILLE
...AND SIMONE

...As narrated by Simone to, and recorded
for posterity by, Katharine Wright

CHAPTER 1

January 1913. Looking Back

As humans go, Will, Orv and their sister Katie have been very kind to me. Normally, I keep a distance from humans because they're dangerous, but long ago I came to love the Wright family. They saved my life, so I've been helping them to understand flying. Considering that humans had always been hopeless at flying, the Wrights have stayed surprisingly interested in it. They're good students—studying, listening, and working hard. They feed me and are gentle with me, and I'm proud of them. So I'd like to tell you our little story.

I'm a herring gull. You'd call me a seagull, although millions of us gulls live quite well all over North America and far from the sea. The Mormon pioneers in Utah even say that the 1848 "Miracle of the Gulls" saved their first harvest and ensured the survival of their Salt Lake City settlement. Pretty neat.

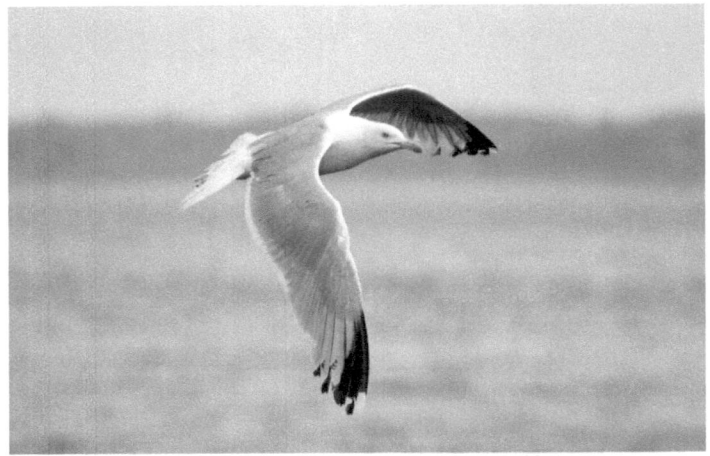

Herring gull
(photo credit: Jalil Arfaoui, via Wikimedia Commons)

Most humans think of birds as dumb. But some of us are actually rather smart. You know that most birds communicate pretty well, in their own ways. We gulls are actually considered noisy. And some birds, such as parrots, mynahs, magpies, mockingbirds and even starlings, can be trained to speak in your English language. Some birds perform in your carnival shows, doing tricks you can't. Obviously, we can fly. We can navigate long distances through the air.

We gulls can float, swim, dive, and catch fish in our mouths. We fly clams up high and drop them down onto rocks to break open their shells. When we get some of your bread, we may drop it as bait on a water surface and then catch the fish that come up for it. You can be taught to swim and dive (your floating is kind of a joke…), but I've never seen a human catch a fish in his mouth. No need to harp on this, and I know you can do a lot of things we can't, but we birds can also do a lot of things you can't. Respect goes both ways. Just sayin'....

So how'd I get mixed-up with the Wrights?

CHAPTER 2

1899. A New Home

> **"Birds are the most perfectly trained gymnasts in the world...specially well fitted for their work."**
>
> *—Wilbur Wright, in his May 30, 1899 letter to the Smithsonian Institution, requesting copies of published work on the subject of human flight*

You've never heard of me. And there are good reasons for that, since enough people already thought the Wright brothers were crazy because they played with kites at their ages (when I met them in 1899, Will was 32 and Orv was 28). But the hints about me were everywhere in what they said in public—especially Will, as in his letter above.

I normally lived and ate around the south shore of Lake Erie, but a violent Canadian storm in early 1899 blew many of us down into central Ohio. As springtime arrived, I found that I liked all the bugs that arose in the rich Ohio farmland, and decided to stay and explore this new place for a while. We don't eat only fish, you know, but eat just about anything that moves (and some that doesn't…).

The Pinnacles, in a gorge south of Dayton, generate nice windy updrafts that make soaring around easy. And between the local farmland and the nearby Great Miami River, there's always plentiful food to catch—even if the place does attract a lot of birds we have to compete with, including those nasty big buzzards (fortunately, they're kind of slow around food, which I think is why they stick to dead stuff…whew!).

One pleasant March day, down below me and standing beside his bicycle, was a human male I'd seen before out here, who seemed to just watch us birds. Elsewhere among the pinnacle rocks were family picnics and kids poking around.

CRACK! Oooow! THUMP! Oooof….

"Back off, boys. I'm Mr. Wilbur Wright—you may know our bicycle shop on West Third Street. You've broken that gull's wing with your slingshot, and you're not going to hurt him anymore. Please help me keep him from flapping away. I'll grab him gently and take him home."

"Golly, Mr. Wright, I didn't mean to hurt him! He just flew by and I took the shot for fun. I've never actually hit a bird before. This is awful! Can you get him to stop screeching? Oh, I didn't mean for this to happen!"

"I understand, son. I was a boy once myself. You just didn't think. But I hope you'll remember this, and never again do things that might hurt animals."

"Yes, Sir! I mean no, Sir. Oh, he just drew blood on your hand! He's a fighter. This is terrible!"

"I've got him now. I'll just wrap him in my scarf, and think I can get him home without any more damage to either of us. You just remember this day. Each of you."

My world had just changed forever.

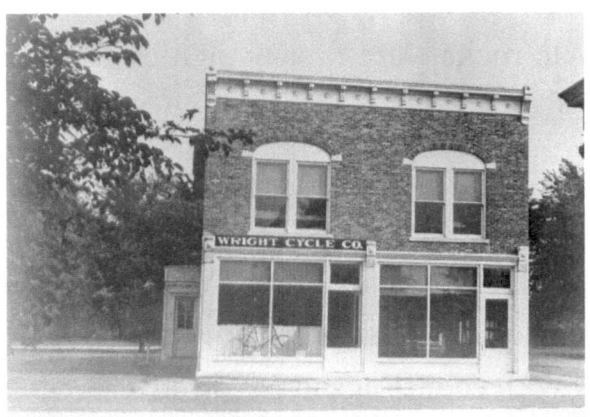

Wright Cycle Company shop, Dayton, Ohio
(photo credit: public domain; Wikimedia
Commons, GPN-2003-00068.jpg)

"Orv, I've got his beak taped so he won't bite you like he bit me. If you can hold his body, I'll try to line up this wing's radial bone, splint it with this little piece of thin molding, and wrap it against his body. These bones are so small and light. Gonna be tough to get this right."

"Oh, hi Katie. Look what I brought home.... We'll try to save him, and hopefully get that wing strong enough that he can eventually fly away free. Do you have some leftover meat we can shred and feed him tonight? I've decided to name him Simon, after the Apostle Simon Peter the fisherman, in the New Testament—son of Jonah."

"Well, big brother, let's begin by understanding that Simon is actually 'Simone.' She's a herring gull, which is the only one with pink legs and black wingtips. She's a girl because she has the white head and breast—with gray on the upper wings and back—of at least a four-year-old adult, but for that age she's smaller than a male. At least she looks pretty healthy. I'll find her some dinner and water, and help you take care of her. Since you guys are mechanics, I suspect that we girls will want to kind of stick together."

"Healthy, Katie? Yup, she sure gives a healthy bite.... For her sake and ours, we'll keep her in this big old bird cage, here in the cycle shop, and see how it goes. I'd appreciate your advice and help, 'cause you know more about these things than I do. Thank you."

Having heard humans speak while scavenging around them much of my life, I realized that these humans, Katie and Will, were talking about me. While humans can hurt you, they're also a great source of junk food (if you're daring and aggressive enough…), so we gulls see and hear them regularly.

As these humans appeared to be trying to help me for some reason, and it looked like I might be in their possession for a while, I decided then and there to pay careful attention to their words and to learn more. It wasn't as if I had anything better to do! We gulls are quick learners, so this could be interesting.

Will left my wing wrapped-up for about 6 weeks, then removed the bandage and carried me out into the yard. By then, I understood that the Wrights were being kind to me. And by then they understood that I wasn't going to bite them. Will set me down in the grass, and I tried to fly. But that broken wing still didn't flap right. And it hurt. I couldn't take off. So Will carried me back into the shop.

"Orv, I don't think I got that wing set properly. Simone may never fly again. We can't just throw her out among the cats and dogs out there. Is it OK with you if we keep her here in the shop for a while longer?"

"Sure, Will. Frankly, as we study the stuff the Smithsonian sent us, and begin our experiments with a kite, I think it's kind of handy to have Simone right here to study how she handles her wings."

Will and Orv were constructing their first serious kite. It looked kind of funny, as all human kites do. This one had two stacked wings held together with wood struts and tight wires.

> **"Everything that can be invented has been invented."**
>
> —*U.S. Commissioner of Patents Charles Duell, 1899*

"You know, Orv, I'd like to design this kite so it doesn't just go up, but with the beginnings of some controls for turning left and right. We could build a rudder on the back, but I'm not sure how we could control that from the ground with string. Any other ideas?"

"Well, Will, how does Simone turn? I think she does it with her wings and tail together."

"That's right," I blurted out.

Two human jaws dropped. Speechless, Will and Orv gawked dumbfounded at me. They looked pretty funny.

"What? You've never seen a bird talk? You two may be more backward country boys than I thought! Look, I really appreciate what you've done for me. But obviously now *you* can use some help, and frankly I'm an expert."

The younger Orv dropped to the floor, out cold.

"Uh. Uh. Uh. Oh…my…gosh."

"Look, Will, it's just a kite. And I can help you. May I?"

"Sure…Simone. Wow. I'm talking to a seagull. A seagull's talking to me. Wow again."

"Come on, Will. You guys already think that a man will learn to fly—which has never been done except in a hot-air balloon or glider. You don't have the muscles for it. I do. Well, I did. There's nothing new about a talking bird. But I can help you get started on this flying thing, and we can see where it goes. I feel like I owe you at least this. Want a suggestion right now for the kite?"

"Geez. Well…yes, I do. How can we make it turn?"

> **"In times of change, learners inherit the Earth, while the learned find themselves beautifully equipped to deal with a world that no longer exists."**
>
> —*American philosopher Eric Hoffer, winner of the Presidential Medal of Freedom*

"When flying, I turn right by lowering the primary feathers near the tip of my left wing. Like this! See?"

"It's kind of like your slightly cupping or twisting your human left hand. As I keep both wings stiff, the passing air raises the left wing and lowers the right wing. And I use my tail to stay balanced during this change, just like the tail on a child's kite keeps it balanced so it won't spin to the ground—you've seen that. Now I'm angled to the right, and the normal lift of my wings causes me to fly—to turn—to the right."

"It's not like the rudder on a boat or the steering wheel on an automobile, because they're not leaning into the turn like me. It's closer to what you do on a bicycle—but still different, partly because you fly in three dimensions, not just two as on the ground. It's actually flying to the right: I have to straighten back up to stop flying to the right. And you have to watch your altitude during the turn, because you're giving-away lift to make the turn."

"There's a lot to it, huh? Now, if you can figure a way to slightly twist your kite's wings, to change their shape like I do, then you'll get the same effect."

"Boy, Simone, there's more to this than I thought. And we're just getting started. You are an expert! And you know what? I'm glad you're here. Thanks!"

As the split bamboo sticks framing this two-wing, five-foot-span kite were made thin to be light, they were also somewhat flexible. So Will and Orv connected four cords going from the kite's leading struts to sticks in their hands on the ground that would enable them to slightly twist the wings in flight.

Will and Orv decided to call this twisting "warping the wings," as recommended by their mentor Octave Chanute. Humans like to play with words, and since I was learning more of their words every day, I just had to deal with their funny habit of saying the same thing different ways. To me, a minnow is a minnow, and I just eat it....

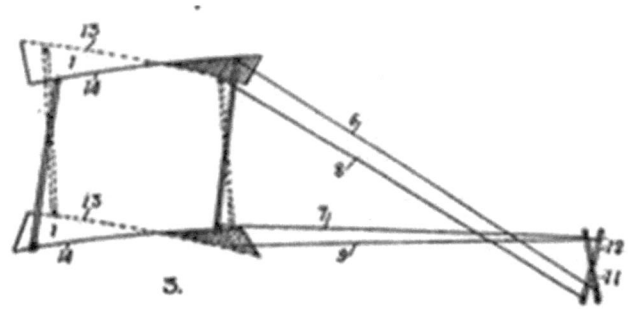

Wilbur's sketch of their 1899 kite
(image credit: Library of Congress,
Prints & Photographs Division)

In early August, Will took this first kite to an open field for a trial. As we were now partners, he let me come along in my cage. I'd considered asking if I might ride on his shoulder, but the Wrights were pretty snazzy dressers all the time, and I didn't want to cramp his style. I mean, the guy wore a necktie to fly a kite! But if I couldn't fly, at least I enjoyed the fresh air and sunshine. And I really enjoyed helping Will and Orv understand what worked for me that might work for them.

As far as neatness and housekeeping go, we agreed that I'd tell them when I needed to go outside to poop, just like a family dog. Except that I could really tell them! So they let me move around in their bicycle shop freely, talk with them at the work benches, and closely examine the stuff they were making. The shop never smelled like fishy poop, which was important to the prim and proper, hard-working, very focused and thoroughly nice Wrights. The shop was the business where they worked—that earned the money they needed to support their experiments. So this was important, and I respected them. A neat seagull—how 'bout that?!

"OK, Simone, the kite's holding altitude. I'm going to warp the wings for a turn."

The kite turned instantly as directed…and then dove directly into the ground. Crunch.

They had a long way to go. No tail. Lack of stability. Look at the bird….

But Will did get his desired turn from this kite, and so "wing-warping" for a turn would carry forward over the next four years into their first flying aeroplane. Of course it worked: just like I told them!

> **"Learning the secret of flight from a bird was a good deal like learning the secret of magic from a magician."**
>
> —*Orville Wright* (He still wasn't willing to say my name, but the magician metaphor was nice....)

CHAPTER 3

1900. Kitty Hawk

During the early months of 1900, Will and Orv decided to find a place somewhere in the country with ideal conditions for kite experiments: (1) steady brisk winds, (2) open area free of obstructions, (3) a hill for launching, and (4) soft sand for landing.

With great help from the United States Weather Bureau, they decided on the tiny fishing village of Kitty Hawk, on the Outer Banks of North Carolina, facing the Atlantic Ocean. (Somehow, they forgot to ask about bugs....) Looking forward to an interesting change of diet, and knowing they'd need my help, I asked to go along, even if having to travel in my cage. They agreed.

In August, we built a big kite with two stacked wings and an 18-foot wingspan, which Will and Orv (here we go again with new words…) decided to call a "glider." Then they took it apart and packed it into crates for the trip to Kitty Hawk.

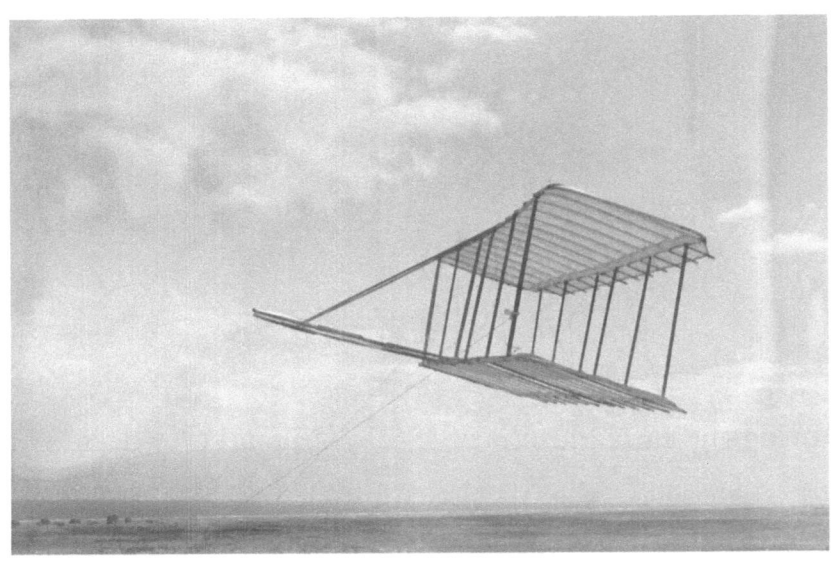

1900 Wright glider
(photo credit: The Library of Congress, Prints &
Photographs Division, LC-DIG-ppprs-00556)

In early September, Will and I took a train from Dayton to Norfolk, Virginia, which was even faster than we gulls could fly such a distance. Now, I was becoming impressed by what these humans could do. It's one thing to fly over a train as it goes by, but something else to ride inside and cover the long distance with no effort at all (and even be fed along the way…). Pretty cool. Another train took us and our crates down to Elizabeth City, North Carolina. Easy.

Then things got exciting. At least for this girl gull.

We had to take a leaky little rowboat for three miles out to a ragged and also leaky old schooner, which then sailed us through awful weather and waves (using what sails didn't break loose…) 40 miles to the Outer Banks and Kitty Hawk. I wouldn't have been out flying in this kind of weather, but trying to survive this in a swinging cage was an experience I hope to never repeat. A seasick seagull is not a pretty sight….

After our crates arrived on another boat, Will put up a tent for us on a sand dune overlooking the ocean. Ah, I'd have loved to fly out there to check out the fishing situation. But fortunately I was soon well-supplied with fresh fish by local boys who often came over to see what this mechanic from Ohio was doing with his "glider." Will and I also enjoyed the fresh sea air and the great view.

By late September, when Orv caught up with us in Kitty Hawk, Will had the glider mostly assembled.

"Will, like I said back in Dayton, that new horizontal wing that you've put on the front of the glider may be fine for helping to get a kite off the ground, but I think what you've really done is put half of the tail in the front. When you get to the point of trying to ride in the glider, that "elevator" as you call it will admittedly help you lift off initially, and probably will help you hold position on the string. But when you take the glider off the string and try to fly free, having half the tail in the front instead of the back is going to make you inherently unstable in the air. You really ought to put all of the tail in the back. Look at me—all of my tail's in the back! And it works. Can you imagine me trying to fly tail-first?"

"Thanks, Simone. I understand. And I appreciate that you're trying to help us. What you say is logical. But we're just starting with the glider on a cord. A bicycle is inherently unstable, too, yet we humans can easily balance and control it while riding. For now, when I think about eventually mounting a glider to fly in it, I still like the idea of having that elevator in the front of the glider to help me quickly prevent and recover from stalls. But I promise you that we'll take another look at the glider design before we try to fly free."

As you can see in any photo of what eventually became the first Wright Flyer, year after year Will and Orv wouldn't let go of that front-mounted elevator idea. They liked the way it helped them get off the ground, and they believed that it helped them recover from stalls. But it made the Flyer naturally unstable in flight—meaning that the pilot had to constantly adjust it to stay in the air. I think it aggravated getting into stalls.

It wasn't until 1910, when the brothers started mass-producing the Wright Model B, that the front-mounted elevator (true to form, humans changed its name to "canard," which is French for the bird "duck") was removed and the elevator was placed in the rear with the rudder (as I'd been recommending all along, since an aeroplane with a duck tied to the front is wrong in so many ways…). Ah, well, I just helped them the best I could!

By October, once the brothers learned to control this big glider-kite so that it would rise no more than about 20 feet above the ground, on days with wind of about 15 miles/hour Will (the only brother who flew during this period), would lie down flat on the lower wing, hold the simple controls, and let the tethered glider lift him off the ground.

To do the wing-warping for turns left and right, the brothers had connected cables from the wingtips to a wood bar on which Will could rest his feet while lying on the lower wing structure—head-first (just like me…) to minimize air resistance on the pilot's body.

"Will," I told him, "you're now beginning to feel the importance of piloting this machine in the air. Flying isn't just about building a gadget with wings that's capable of rising up. I was born with wings, and never had any control over how I was built. And when I first stepped to the edge of the nest, I knew nothing about flying. What I had to learn from watching my parents and trial and error, starting as a young chick, was how to handle my 'equipment' in the air—and in my case also on and under water. Hah—let's hope your glider never ends-up on water!"

"Please remember that your machine wants to fall out of the sky any chance it gets. You must learn not only to control it every second—so that it doesn't hurt you—but also to sense what else it might do for you as you expand your own piloting skills."

"Only a fraction of flying is 'equipment.' The majority of flying is piloting. That means you, not the machine. You're eventually going to have to learn about, feel, and act to handle things like balance side-to-side and fore-and-aft, taking off, landing, wind gusts, crosswinds, thermals, downdrafts, glide ratio, stalling and recovery, mountain-wave effect near cliffs and hills, turning about a point on the ground, navigating over the ground without getting lost, dealing with clouds and storms, darkness—so much to learn!"

"I can help you with all this stuff. Been there, done that."

"Starting right now, always be thinking out ahead of that glider. What's out there? What's it about to do? Make yourself ready to handle what's coming. When you get to the point of really flying free, it's all about keeping your mind way out ahead of where you are."

"But I shouldn't get ahead of myself. Don't want to throw too much at you before you're ready. I mean, you haven't yet told me how you plan to make your future flyer flap its wings so it can take off under its own power!"

"By the way, are you planning to make a bunch of them and fly in a flock? That introduces another whole area of thinking: how to avoid running into each other."

"At least you're not planning to use your eventual flyer to get your food like we birds do...are you?"

"Sometimes, when humans are throwing bread up to us on the beach, we get a kick out of dropping our poop down onto their heads. Gets a great reaction! Maybe, some day, when you eventually learn to fly, you humans might want to think about things you could drop. But I digress...."

When we weren't out flying the glider, we talked at length about many aspects of glider design and piloting. Will and Orv were attentive students to what we birds know and do. And since I couldn't fly for them, I often asked them to go outside and look for some of the many local birds doing what I was talking about.

> **They'd stand on the beach for hours at a time just looking at the gulls flying, soaring, dipping.... They would watch the gannets and imitate the movements of their wings with their arms and hands. They could imitate every movement of the wings of those gannets; we thought they were crazy, but we just had to admire the way they could move their arms this way and that and bend their elbows and wrist bones up and down and which way, just like the gannets.**
>
> *—Kitty Hawk Life-Saving Station #7 member John T. Daniels*

The gannets that Mr. Daniels was talking about were the largest seabirds around Kitty Hawk, with a wingspan up to six feet—thus easy to watch. But they're gross eaters, "gannet" being an old English synonym for "glutton." It is fun to watch them dive from high in the air and strike the water as fast as 62 miles per hour, which means they can catch fish deeper than me. But I think all that concussion on their heads makes them not too bright. No wonder they're in the scientific genus Morus (moron...), and closely related to the blue-footed booby. No kidding!

By the 19th of October, Will was ready to try flying the glider off a hill, without the kite string. A real glider, not a glider-kite. This was exciting! We moved four miles south from Kitty Hawk to the three Kill Devil Hills.

As Will was preparing himself for his first real gliding flight off "Big Hill," I reminded him, "Will, gliding off the string is a whole new level of piloting for you. This won't be just up and down and a little sideways. You can rise too fast and stall much harder than on a kite string. You won't necessarily land gently, because you can be going 30 miles per hour when you touch the ground, and both the fore-and-aft and lateral attitudes of the glider must be just right. Just as I did as a chick, take your time…feel your way…go slow."

"For you, slow is fast, because if you break the glider, or worse break some of your own bones, you're done for this season. Orv and Bill Tate there will be helping you get launched down that hillside, but once airborne it's all you, the pilot in the air."

"Have situational awareness all around, be sensitive to everything around you, and be decisive in responding to any surprises. There will be surprises. They'll happen fast, and they'll need quick and delicate response. You'll tend to overreact in the air, so be conservative in what you try at every step."

From Big Kill Devil Hill, Will made his first free glider flight. Then he did it again and again. He glided as far as

400 feet. Even though I have flown for hundreds of miles, I loved the excitement on the face of this beginning pilot, whose courage was clear as he flew again and again, carefully and safely.

As the ever-helpful Bill Tate, who also happened to be Kitty Hawk's postmaster, liked to say, **"We believed that God did not intend man should ever fly**." And certainly, from a gull's point of view, the human body is barely useful for swimming and looks utterly hopeless for flying. But here was Will Wright gliding through the air over and over. Even for me, it was thrilling.

By late October we'd accomplished what we wanted to do in this Kitty Hawk season, and headed home to Dayton. This gull felt good. Will and Orv, in their quiet way, were deservedly ecstatic. Nobody else knew it yet, but they were already among the most accomplished aeronautical engineers and pilots in the human world.

> "We were very much pleased with the general results of the trip, for setting out as we did, with almost revolutionary theories on many points, and an entirely untried form of machine, we considered it quite a point to be able to return without having our pet theories completely knocked in the head...and our own brains dashed out in the bargain."
>
> —Wilbur Wright

Of course, compared to what a two-month-old gull knows and can do...well, I just politely held my tongue. You have to be patient with humans—especially when they're feeding you....

> **"What use is a new-born baby?"**—*Benjamin Franklin, November 21, 1783, in Paris after signing the Treaty of Paris that successfully ended the American Revolutionary War. While witnessing the first free (untethered) balloon flight by man—de Rozier and d'Arlandes in a Montgolfier hot-air balloon—Mr. Franklin was asked by a skeptical fellow spectator what use was such a thing, and this was his reply.*

CHAPTER 4

1901. Frustration and Renewal

Over the winter of 1900-1901, we had decided that our next step would be to build a larger glider along the same design, except with a greater curvature in the wings. Of course, always playing with words, Will and Orv decided to call this curvature in the wings "camber." Camber in the Wright's cloth wings at this point was expressed as the height of the wing curve over its chord length, the chord being a straight line from leading edge to trailing edge.

Will and Orv also added a new "hip cradle" to move the wing-warping wires, with the benefit that the pilot would no longer need to make the awkward foot movements to do wing-warping.

Our second glider turned out to be the biggest glider ever built, which was kind of neat. By June, with this glider almost completed, Will and Orv decided that we'd head to Kitty Hawk in July, leaving the Wright Cycle Company in the care of newly-hired machinist Charlie Taylor who, I later learned, would play a key role in the first-ever Wright Flyer aeroplane.

On July 7th, with the usual crates of glider stuff, we were on the train to North Carolina.

This time, we built our camp at Kill Devil Hills. Will and Orv built a shed hangar to protect the big glider, and we lived in it. We were joined by helpers Mr. Ed Huffaker from Tennessee and Mr. George Spratt from Pennsylvania, so the food handouts that came my way increased nicely! And old Mr. Octave Chanute came to visit—the mentor whom Will and Orv listened to carefully, as he was widely respected among humans interested in flight.

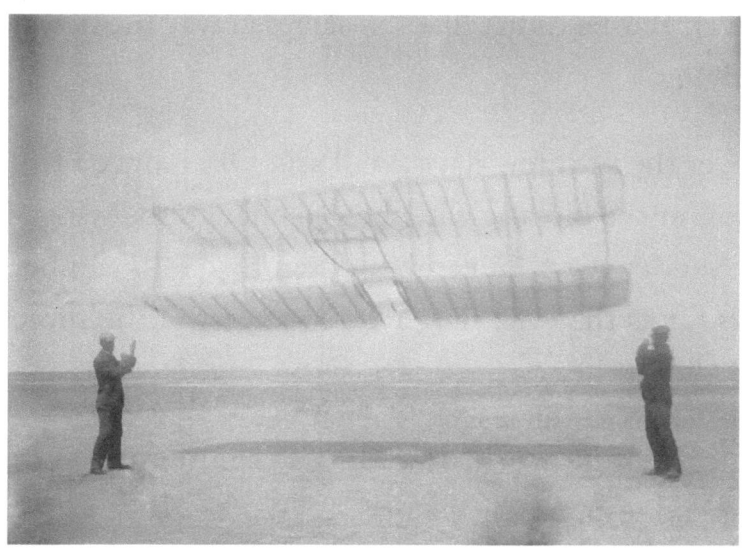

1901 Wright glider
(photo credit: Library of Congress, Prints & Photographs Division, LC-DIG-ppprs-00571)

On July 27th, Will made his first flight in the big glider. Well, it wasn't much of a flight. Just after lift-off, the glider dove into the ground. I told Will to slide farther back on the wing, since the greater camber obviously greatly changed its flying characteristics.

After a couple more changes in his position, he finally glided 300 feet, and I reminded him that free flying means that even subtle changes to a wing can make a big difference and require him to make immediate but delicate adjustments. Control in flight requires great concentration and immediate decisiveness—with a delicate touch.

With steadily-increasing experience, Will was becoming a believer. But he didn't like the sluggish way the new glider was flying.

So, over the next few days, Will and Orv reduced the wire tension in the biplane wing box to change the wings from their very curvy 1-12 camber down to a 1-19 camber, but not as far as the even flatter 1-23 camber of the successful 1900 glider-kite.

This flattening worked, and Will again got the easily-controlled response he wanted.

Until August 9th. According to Will, as he was landing at speed the left wing snagged the sand and the glider crashed into the ground, injuring Will's face and chest. As it then rained for days and Will got a cold, on August 20th we just headed home.

Will and Orv were frustrated by all the things they didn't understand. I tried to help, but frankly that big wood and cloth glider was so different from my own experience that there was a lot that I didn't understand about it, either.

I did remind them, however, that I had a quite helpful tail, and their confusing glider did not. Glumly, they said they'd think about it. It's good that I'm not a chicken, because these dejected men would probably have accused me of "hen-pecking" them....

> **"We doubted that we would ever resume our experiments.... At this time, I made the prediction that men would sometime fly, but it would not be in our lifetime."**
>
> —*Wilbur, August 1901, about the train ride home*
>
> (Yup, when we got home I had some serious cheerleading to do—although I was tempted to agree with him. After all, these guys were only human....)

Back in Dayton, Will and Orv decided that their control problems came partly from depending on the scientific data about lift, balance and steering of earlier investigators such as their American friend Octave Chanute and a Prussian named Otto Lilienthal who had died from injuries in an 1896 glider accident—after gliding a record 820 feet earlier the same day.

To Lilienthal's great credit, by the way, in 1889 he had published a book titled *Bird Flight as the Basis of Aviation.* Must've been a very smart man! In fact, in September 1909 while flying from Tempelhof Aerodrome in Berlin, Orville visited Lilienthal's widow to pay his respects.

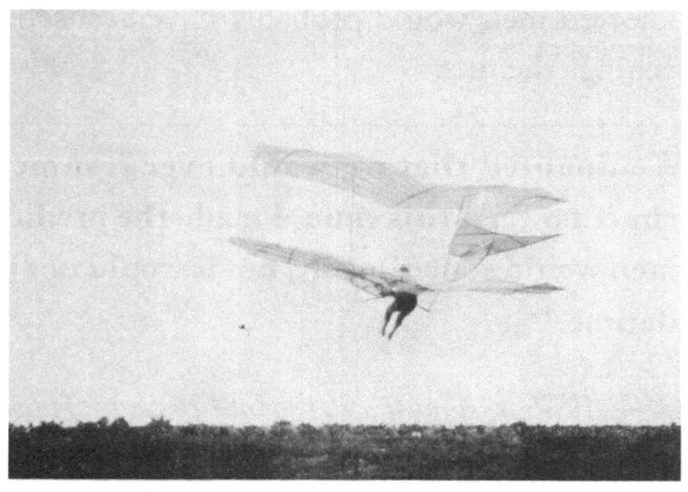

1895 Otto Lilienthal glider
(photo credit: Library of Congress, Prints &
Photographs Division, LC-DIG-ppprs-00586)

The brilliant and wealthy civil engineer Chanute, still very much engaged with the Wrights, was the designer and lead builder of many important bridges in the United States, including the first bridge in Kansas City over the Missouri River (which is quite popular with local gulls). He even designed the nation's two largest stock yards, which have contributed greatly to the economies of Kansas City and Chicago. My gull friends from up along Lake Michigan tell me that the Chicago stock yards are a pretty interesting place to eat....

It was Chanute's "strut-wire" biplane wing structure—based on the Pratt truss used in bridges—that the Wrights adapted in each glider they made—using bicycle spoke wire because they had it handy!

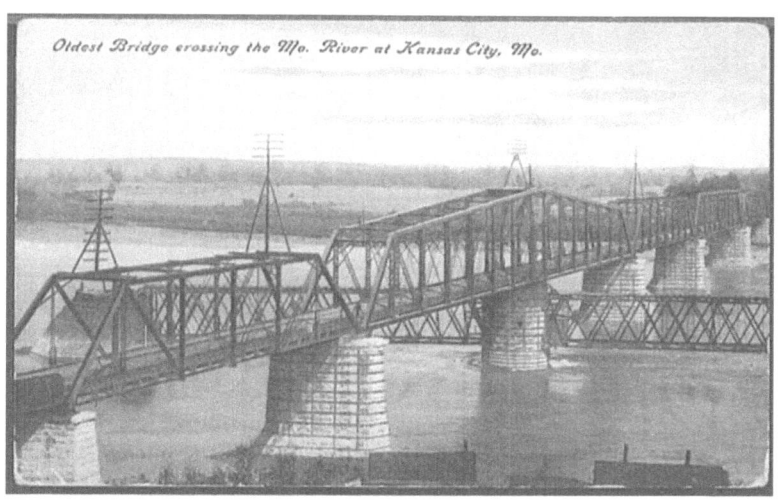

Oldest Bridge crossing the Mo. River at Kansas City, Mo.

Chanute's original 1869 Hannibal Bridge
at Kansas City, using the Pratt truss

(image credit: public domain via
Wikimedia Commons)

But this earlier data, such as Lilienthal's recommended 1-12 camber, just wasn't working for them. So Will and Orv decided that they would do their own experiments on wing and flight control design—and would develop their own objective data that should work for them.

> **"We saw that the calculations upon which all flying machines had been based were unreliable, and that all were simply groping in the dark. Having set out with absolute faith in the existing scientific data, we were driven to doubt one thing after another, till finally, after two years of experiment, we cast it all aside, and decided to rely entirely on our own investigations."**
>
> —Wilbur Wright

That autumn, with their guidance, machinist Charlie Taylor built them a 6-foot-long wooden wind tunnel, and Orv designed lift and drag measuring "balances" for it—made from hacksaw blades and bicycle spokes. They tested scores of airfoil shapes, and different angles of attack, recording and graphing the most useful data. No human (or bird...) had ever done such a thorough scientific study.

At this point in our friendship, I didn't want to bias their thinking by talking about birds (over 60 species of which, such as ostriches and penguins, can't fly at all...), so I just quietly let them build their experimental tables of numbers. It gave them wonderful confidence as they learned patiently and steadily for themselves what worked and what didn't. I was proud of them again.

CHAPTER 5

1902. Great Progress

On August 26th, our third glider in crates, we departed Dayton for Kitty Hawk.

Built upon the many lessons Will and Orv had learned during their winter experiments, this new glider had a longer, narrower 32-foot wingspan (shaped much more like mine, which are efficient for gliding…).

Since wing camber was still to be experimented-with on the new glider, Will and Orv smartly designed the wings' supporting wires to be adjustable in the field, with a wing camber range from 1-24 down flatter to 1-30. Yet again, their mechanical experience with building bicycles and their scientific, always-learning approach gave our project added flexibility to make rapid progress as experimental flights proceeded.

And—the best part at long last!—for increased stability this glider had at least the vertical part of a tail, which they called a rudder, even if it didn't move. For a herring gull, the scale of this thing was getting pretty spectacular, but I knew they'd eventually figure out the need for that two-finned rudder to help them steer—meaning that they'd have to make it movable.

Getting the elevator moved from front to the back, as I recommended, they just wouldn't understand. They were convinced that the front elevator was essential for preventing or recovering from stalls. I told them that, if you put the elevator in the tail, most of your stall problem will go away— because you won't be over-correcting with it so much! Will having now taught himself to depend on that front elevator, he just couldn't accept my argument. You do what you can....

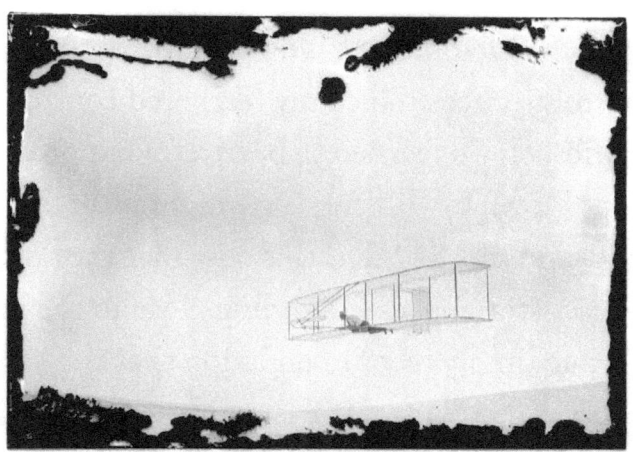

1902 Wright glider with fixed rudder

(photo credit: Library of Congress, Prints & Photographs Division, LC-DIG-ppprs-00630)

On September 19th, we test-flew this glider as a kite from a hill near Kitty Hawk. Satisfied with that, we moved the four miles to the Kill Devil Hills. Then Will—and for the first time Orv—flew it as a free glider over 40 times.

I could see that Will, with his experience over the past two seasons, was now a much surer hand at the controls than the beginner Orv. The "feel" that I'd told them about was really paying off. But Will was also a patient teacher and a loving brother, as the two spent their usual long days working side-by-side to learn and improve their results. Following my early advice, they thought through each step of their flights, didn't over-extend themselves, and except for minor accidents were careful and safe. What a pleasure being part of this team!

The evening of October 2nd, we got into another long talk about control surfaces. Since my feathered control surfaces were so different, I'd learned to be careful but precise in my suggestions for what Will and Orv might want to do to this huge wood-and-cloth glider. But now that they'd regained confidence in straight-ahead gliding close to the ground, I brought up again my recommendation that they'd get a lot more stability and control if they put the entire tail in the back, instead of the "elevator" half of the tail in the front.

Orville compromised with me, saying that he still liked the front elevator to help prevent nose-dives after takeoff, but that he could see the logic of having a swinging vertical rudder in the back—movable just like my tail—to help with turning, especially as the glider flew higher.

The next morning, Will not only agreed to go along with the swinging rudder in the back, but said why not coordinate rudder movement and wing-warping for turns by connecting both controls to the hip cradle? Everybody agreed.

Wow. Will and Orv had just accepted the idea of the "coordinated turn," which of course I'd been doing all my flying life.

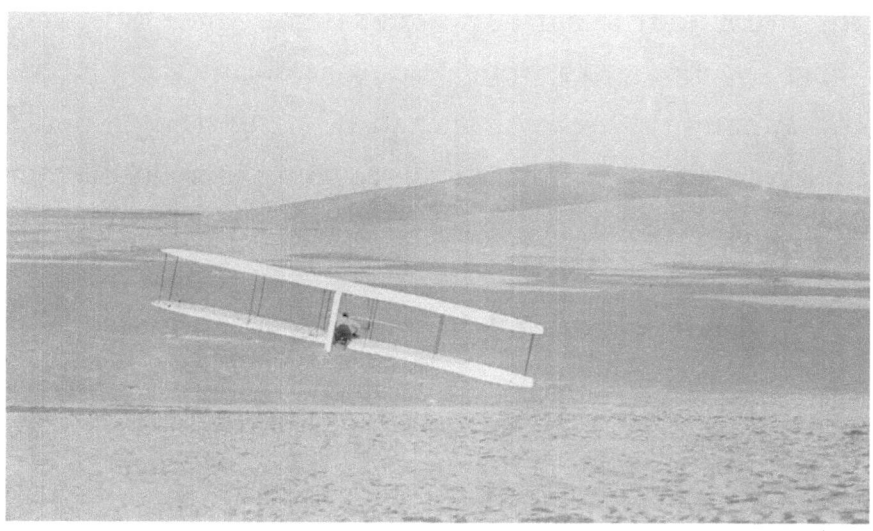

1902 Wright glider with movable rudder
(photo credit: Library of Congress, Prints & Photographs Division, LC-DIG-ppprs-00598)

On October 17th, we took the improved big glider to Kill Devil Hills. It had a moving single rudder in the back, which had replaced the earlier fixed twin rudder. When you look at Will and Orv's photographs from 1902, the rudder easily tells you which version of the 1902 glider you're looking at.

Will and Orv now flew many times each day under vastly-improved control, ranging out as far as 600 feet.

By October 28th when we headed home, they had made over 900 glides this season. Will and Orv were successful, proven, reliable and confident glider pilots.

They were ready to pursue powered flight. These guys were impressive mechanics, world-leading aeronautical engineers, and apparently the best human pilots on the planet. I couldn't wait to see how they were going to make 32-foot wings flap....

> **"Heavier-than-air flying machines are impossible"**
>
> —*Famous British scientist Lord Kelvin,*
> *President of the Royal Society, 1895*

CHAPTER 6

1903. Powered Flight

Will and Orv decided that they'd try to power their glider with one of those noisy, smelly new gasoline engines, with two wooden fans called "propellers" connected to the engine by chains and sprocket gears much like those on a bicycle, which they understood as well as anyone.

From their studies, they calculated that their aeroplane would require an engine that could produce 8 horsepower and weigh no more than 200 pounds, creating 90 pounds of thrust in order to push their estimated 625 pounds of plane and pilot through the air at least 23 miles/hour.

Approaching a number of manufacturers of automobile engines during these early years of the automobile, the Wrights found that those companies couldn't be bothered to make just one such specialized product. So they turned to their employee: machinist and bicycle mechanic Charlie

Taylor. Now, I'm clueless about such things, but what Charlie then accomplished really did impress me.

> **"My only experience with a gasoline engine was an attempt to repair one in an automobile in 1901."**
>
> —*Charles E. Taylor*

Will, Orv and Charlie would coordinate in making hand-drawn diagrams of various engine parts they wanted, and Charlie would machine these parts from either factory castings or raw metal using the same lathe and drill press that he used to make bicycles.

In just six weeks, Charlie produced a 4-cylinder, water-cooled, 12 horsepower, 180-pound engine with an innovative (light) aluminum crankcase, which operated with no fuel pump (gravity-fed from a 22-ounce fuel tank hung on a strut), no carburetor (simple fuel-air mix chamber next to the cylinders), no onboard battery or spark plugs (a magneto plus two bicycle chain/cam-operated contact points in each cylinder), and no throttle (constant speed).

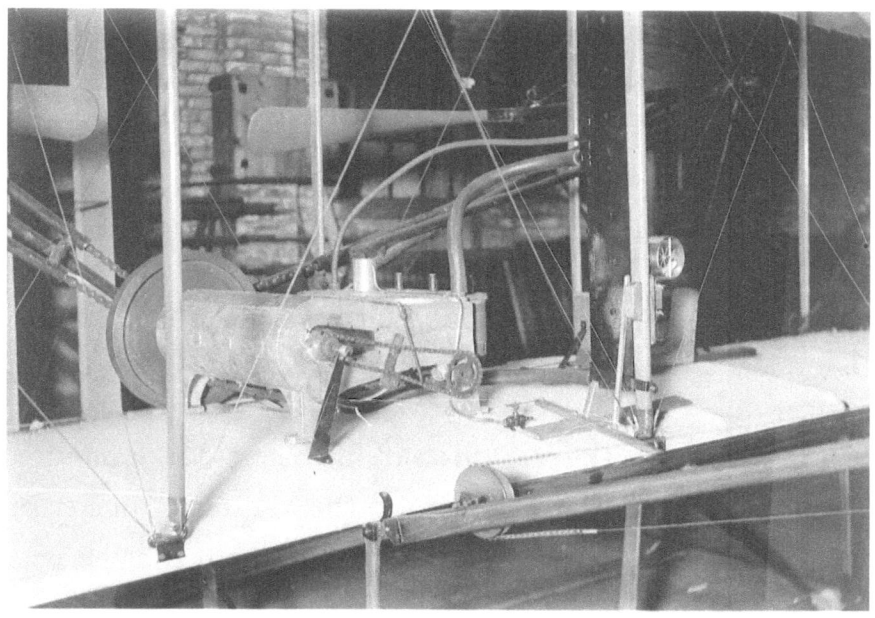

Wright Flyer I engine
(photo credit: Library of Congress, Prints &
Photographs Division, LC-DIG-ppprs-00651)

Finding no scientific papers available to describe mathematically how propellers worked, including from the U.S. Navy, Will again did wind-tunnel tests. He became convinced that propellers were actually rotating wings, and from this understanding personally hand-carved (with a hatchet and drawknife) the two 8.5-foot-long laminated spruce wood propellers. Installed on the aeroplane, the brothers made them counter-rotate—to eliminate torque that would make the machine try to turn—simply by twisting the chain to one of them 180 degrees!

On March 23rd, Will and Orv applied for a federal patent on what later became known as the Wright Flyer I, and specifically on their wing-warping apparatus (the principle of which I taught them...) and their moving rudder in the rear (not to brag, but you know...).

However, this engine-burdened heavy machine hadn't flown yet.

On June 24th, on the invitation of his friend Mr. Chanute, Will gave a speech in Chicago to the Western Society of Engineers. Obviously, he couldn't tell them that he was being advised by a herring gull (the gulls around Chicago's Lake Michigan shore weren't especially appreciated...), as well as patenting ideas that he'd learned from a talking bird. But he did give a lot of credit to the brothers' study of birds and—as he now appreciated from both my advice and his own experience—the importance of experience in actually piloting through the air. He told them:

Before trying to rise to any dangerous height a man ought to know that in an emergency his mind and muscles will work by instinct rather than conscious effort. There is no time to think.... The birds' wings are undoubtedly very well designed indeed, but it is not any extraordinary efficiency that strikes with astonishment but rather the marvelous skill with which they are used.... The soaring problem is

apparently not so much one of better wings as of better operators.

Right on! You da man!

On September 23rd, we headed to North Carolina, following the crated parts of what Will and Orv called their "Whopper Flying Machine"...now up to a 40-foot wingspan with a 1-20 camber—that had been sent ahead on an earlier train. Interestingly, the Whopper was so big that it had never been fully assembled in Dayton.

During our first week at Kitty Hawk, and with the ever-helpful Dan Tate, the brothers built a new 16 x 44-foot hangar to protect the Whopper. They finished this hangar just in time to protect the plane from a gale packing winds up to 75 miles per hour.

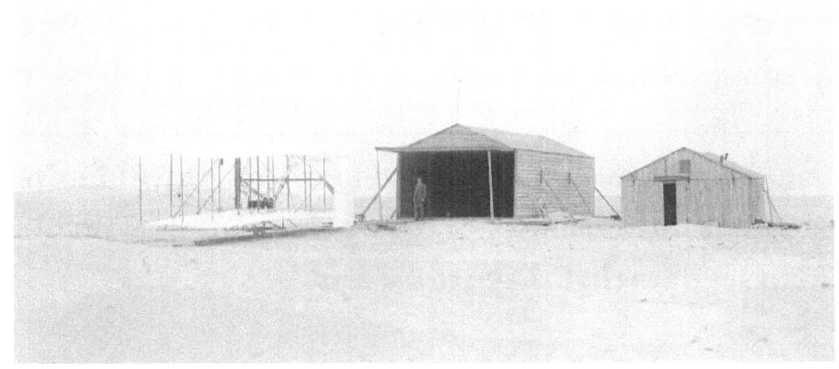

1903 Wright hangar at Kill Devil Hills
(photo credit: Library of Congress, Prints &
Photographs Division, LC-DIG-ppprs-00607)

Weather continued to be a challenge. Although the Whopper was assembled by early November, a misfiring engine test bent the steel tubing propeller shafts, which had to be sent by railroad back to Charlie in Dayton to be replaced.

While we waited, we suffered through a lot of rain, and then ice, and then snow—on top of the usual wind.

Then, after the new stronger tube steel shafts arrived and were tested, they cracked! This engine thing was making our work at Kitty Hawk a lot harder, slower, and certainly frustrating! But on November 30th Orv headed back to Dayton to try again.

Note to self: Working hard and smart is key to success. But perseverance in the face of adversity is essential, if not much fun…. The Wright Brothers really had it—and they certainly needed it. Being a bird is easier! (if some human is feeding you….)

"Airplanes suffer from so many technical faults that it is only a matter of time before any reasonable man realizes that they are useless."

—*Scientific American magazine, 1910*

On December 11th, Orv arrived in Kitty Hawk with new solid steel propeller shafts...a hard lesson learned for all future aeroplane builders.

On December 14th, with help by some of the guys from the Life-Saving Station at the nearby beach, the brothers hauled the heavy 605-pound (empty weight) Whopper to Big Hill, where they placed their new 60-foot-long wood launch rail on a gentle slope to boost the first test launch.

After the Whopper was made ready, Will won a coin toss with Orv and crawled into position on the lower wing. Engine howling, and with Orv balancing the wings, the Whopper tottered down the launch rail and floated up until Will pulled too hard on that darned elevator, lifting the nose too high, then overcompensated and slammed the Whopper into the ground about 100 feet later.

Fortunately, there was only a little damage to the Whopper, which had actually worked nicely. Will had made a pilot error because this heavy craft was new to him. He didn't have the feel yet.

I resisted the temptation to chastise him for still having half the tail in the front of the plane. It was time to encourage Will and Orv, so that's what I did. "Hang in there, guys. You can do this! You've just flown 112 feet. It wasn't really controlled, but you'll get the feel of it...."

A cold wind blew on Thursday morning, December 17th. The Whopper was repaired. The brothers signaled that they were ready, and five men came up from the Life-Saving Station to help move the aeroplane out to a new launching point on level ground.

It was Orville's turn to fly, so Will balanced the wings while the single-speed engine warmed up.

At 10:35 a.m. on December 17th, the Whopper began to trundle down the launch rail into a gusty headwind of 21 miles/hour. Will could run with it, balancing a wing, until it rose into the air about 40 feet down the launch rail. Now truly the Wright Flyer, it erratically flew 120 feet in 12 seconds.

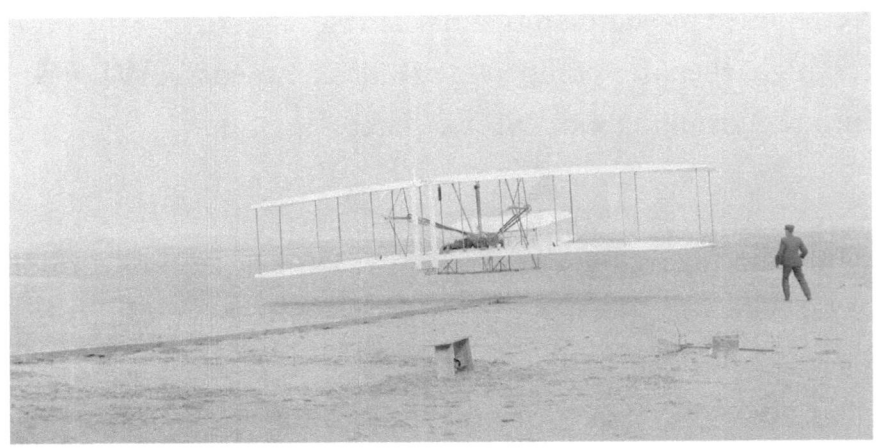

10:35 a.m. December 17, 1903. First flight

This photo was taken on Will's camera by Life-Saving Station #7 member John T. Daniels

(photo credit: The Library of Congress, Prints & Photographs Division, LC-DIG-pprs-00626)

> "This flight lasted only 12 seconds, but it was nevertheless the first in the history of the world in which a machine carrying a man had raised itself by its own power into the air in full flight, had sailed forward without reduction of speed, and had finally landed at a point as high as that from which it had started."
>
> —Pilot Orville Wright

A man, for the first time in history, had **piloted a controlled, sustained flight in a heavier-than-air powered aircraft.**

Later in the morning, Will and Orv alternated flying. In the fourth flight, Will flew 852 feet in 59 seconds—seven times the distance of the first flight. Clearly, mankind had an impressive capacity to quickly advance this new science of aeronautics, and mankind was on its way!

It was enough to make a gull proud.

You know, people always talk about the Wright Flyer as if the machine is what it's all about. But I was even more proud of the courage, skill, and accomplishments of my two pleasant necktie-wearing friends (yes, even on these first flights!), who were teaching the world how important the piloting is.

As the brothers talked of another launch, a wind gust suddenly blew the Flyer—and 200-pound John T. Daniels—tumbling down the beach, badly damaging it (and him). Wow, historic success and then another disaster....

As they say nowadays, "Flying today is completed." You move on.

After lunch, Will and Orv walked to Kitty Hawk and sent a telegram to Dayton. When *Dayton Daily Journal* city editor Frank Tunison read their telegram (59 seconds having been mistransmitted as 57), he famously responded, "Fifty-seven seconds, eh? If it had been 57 minutes, then it might have been a news item." His newspaper did not report it, but the competing *Dayton Daily News* reported the Dayton citizens' accomplishment on an inside page.

In contrast, as an indicator of the questionable accuracy of some 1903 journalism—and maybe local speculation about potential tourist business—the Norfolk *Virginian-Pilot* headlined, "FLYING MACHINE SOARS 3 MILES IN TEETH OF HIGH WIND OVER HILLS AND WAVES AT KITTY HAWK ON CAROLINA COAST."

AFTERWORD

There is, of course, a lot more to the story of the Wright brothers—some of it great fun and colored with royalty… some of it full of hard work and more frustration…much of it about great achievements and even more disaster. But you can find all that elsewhere in recollections far better than those of a grounded herring gull. My most important story with the Wright family was at the beginning, and now you have it.

I have shared my story with the encouragement and help of the darling Katie Wright—who herself flew alongside her brother Will multiple times, once in front of King Edward VII of England. Katie was the third woman in the world to fly in an aeroplane, and is one of the few American women to be awarded the Government of France's Légion d'Honneur. Katie served as an officer in the Wright Company, was key to their successful sales efforts in Europe, and cared for the gravely injured Orville after his September 17, 1908 crash at Fort Myer, Virginia.

In the future, I think you will see more human females not only flying in aeroplanes, but piloting them: another obvious lesson from the success of birds....

Love, Simone

January 25, 1913

"When once you have tasted flight, you will forever walk the Earth with your eyes turned skyward, for there you have been, and there you will always long to return."

—*Leonardo da Vinci*